PREPARING for BATTLE

Exploring Ephesians 6

Vic Reasoner

3080 Brannon Rd
Nicholasville, KY 40356-9700

ISBN 979-8-9937696-8-4

TABLE of CONTENTS

PREPARING for BATTLE
Introduction

Acts 19 records Paul's visit to Ephesus on his third missionary journey. There he encountered black magic, cult religion, and demonic power. Ephesians contains more about these principalities and power than any other New Testament letter. In reaction to this spiritual warfare, Paul emphasizes the power of God more in this epistle than any of his other writings.

As he brings the Ephesian letter to a close he explains that there is opposition to God's plan. There is a cosmic conflict in progress. Paul issues a call to arms. There is no possibility that God's plan will fail but we can be defeated if we do not understand the battle we are in.

Ephesians 6:10-13 reveals that we have an adversary. Flesh and blood — a reference to humanity — is not our enemy but people may be puppets of the enemy — the devil.

We need to know two things about our enemy. First, our enemy is organized.

- *rulers* are arch-demons — the first in order and rank
- *authorities* are the next level down
- *cosmic power* describes the function of demons to infiltrate systems of power.
- *spiritual forces of evil* may be a general term for all evil spirits.

These levels may be hard to distinguish because they work through human structures. Demons have infiltrated political systems and every structure not under the lordship of Christ. According to 1 John 5:19, "the whole world is under the control of the evil one."

Don't become obsessed or paranoid. C. S. Lewis warned,

> There are two equal and opposite errors into which our race can fall about devils. One is to disbelieve in their existence. The other is to believe, and to feel an excessive and unhealthy interest in them. They themselves are equally pleased by both errors and hail a materialist or a magician [superstition] with the same delight.[1]

Second, our enemy is crafty or wily. The Greek word used is μεθοδεία (*methodeia*). However, it is actually a neutral word meaning the following after a way. It connotes a system, a scheme, a strategy, or organization. It is the basis for our English word *method*. Thus, we could say that the devil was the first Methodist!

The term *Methodist* originated as a derogatory nickname at Oxford University for John Wesley and his brother Charles, along with fellow students, who were mocked for their highly disciplined, "methodical" approach to Christian living, including strict Bible study, prayer schedules, and charitable work, earning them the label "Holy Club"" and "Methodists" as an insult.

Methodist discipleship understands that our enemy has a scheme to defeat us. We must fight fire with fire. If we have no spiritual disciplines, we are sitting ducks. We must have a

---

[1]Lewis, *Screwtape Letters*, 3.

method and the Methodist method involved appropriating the means of grace which include conferencing and accountability. In 1971 Charles Ferguson wrote a history of American Methodism entitled *Organizing to Beat the Devil*.

Notice in v 13 *the evil day*. The fight is perpetual but some days more intense. This is what we mean when we say "when it rains it pours." We prepare for such evil days by remaining vigilant even when things are going well.

A great crisis was soon approaching. Paul was writing in AD 61-62. The six years 64-70 extend from the fire of Rome to the fall of Jerusalem. Persecution would soon be unleashed on the young church.

We not only have an adversary, we have an advocate (1 John 2:1). According to Ephesians 1:21, Jesus Christ is above all the good angels and fallen angels referenced in 6:12.

We fight from a position of strength. Christ has won, but he allows us to fight. We must make his strength our own. We must appropriate what God has provided. Jesus has provided all the protection we need, but we must utilize it.

Why does Paul refer to our spiritual protection as *armor*? Look at v 20. Paul is chained to a Roman guard. Paul describes our armor in the same sequence that the guard would have dressed. As he looks at that Roman guard he does not cower, but the Holy Spirit shows him that he too is armed.

How to Interpret the Armor

This is a vivid allegory of the Christian armor and conflict. The term *allegory* means that a comparison is being made through symbolism. The danger is that interpret the symbol to mean whatever we assume it meant before we gave it consideration. God actually wants us to think about it. But we can overthink it.

> The six pieces of armor here named, which include girdle and sandals, are sufficiently explained by the writer himself, and ought not, in interpretation, to be pressed into all possible details of comparison which corresponding portions of ancient armor might be made to suggest.[2]

John Calvin also cautioned against putting too much emphasis on the detail of each piece of armor, since all that Paul intended was an analogy.[3] In 1655 William Gurnall published *The Christian in Complete Armor*. The most recent reprint runs 1200 pages. Adam Clarke wrote that it "contains a great many excellences; but surely it does not require such a volume to explain the *five* verses of this chapter."[4]

Paul's letters all divide into a doctrinal section and an application. This armor analogy is located in the practical section. Some commentators interpret much of the armor as objective propositions. For example, Calvinistic commentators often interpret the breastplate of righteousness as the imputed righteousness of Christ. In contrast Adam Clarke said it was living a holy life. While I affirm these doctrines, I don't think that is Paul's emphasis. Instead, he is teaching the believer the practical application of these doctrines. Now that you are born again, how do you deal with doubt, with depression, with distraction? How do we connect knowledge and vital piety?

Yes, Paul taught justification by faith and his starting point was Habbakuk 2:2-4. But not only are we made righteous,

---

[2]Terry, *Biblical Hermeneutics*, 316-317.

[3]Calvin, *Commentary*, 21:338.

[4]Clarke, *Commentary*, 6:473.

those who have been justified are to *live* by faith. As Paul discusses the analogy of armor he is teaching subjectively how we live the Christian life victoriously.

On the spectrum of belief, at the more charismatic side, is the battle won by affirmation of positional truth or must there be active confrontation with the forces of darkness? In all these questions the correct position is a balance. However, Hank Hanegraaff wrote, "The tragedy today is that multitudes suppose that righteousness can be achieved through deliverance, rather than through discipleship."[5]

And so Paul says all Christians have

- a belt
- a breastplate
- shoes
- a shield
- a helmet
- a sword

How do we put them on? In the song, "Stand up, stand up for Jesus" we sing "Put on the gospel armor, each piece put on with prayer."[6] Such an army of meek cannot be stopped. They will inherit the earth. If we appropriate all the protection God has provided, we will still be standing when the battle is over.

---

[5]Hanegraaff, *The Covering*, 59.

[6]George Duffield (1858).

For Discussion

Tension and stress will come from relationships. The grass may look greener across the fence, but those we do not know also deal with tension and stress in their relationships. Every extended family is dysfunctional, beginning with Adam and Eve failing to accept responsibility for their sins and the tension between Cain and Abel.

There will be tension over politics, over money, over culture, over race, over religion. But the real culprit is always the devil who knows how to instigate conflict.

We are thrown off balance by doubt, accusation, resentment, confusion, depression, and temptation. What tool has the devil been trying to use on you?

The Freedom of a Belt
Ephesians 6:14

The first piece of equipment was the belt. Literally the text says *Stand, having gird your loins with truth*. The participle περιζώννυμι (*perizonnumi*) means to gird all around.

This belt was not used to hold up trousers. In Bible times no one wore trousers. They wore loose-fitting robes to protect them from the sun while allowing airflow and the evaporation of sweat. But you cannot run, or work, or fight in those loose-fitting robes, so they must be cinched or gird up by tucking them into a belt or girdle around the waist. The equivalent today would be to take off your jacket, loosen our tie, or roll up your sleeves.

The Bible uses this metaphor in 1 Peter 1:13 which literally says to gird up the loins of your mind. The ESV says prepare your mind for action. In Luke 12:35 Jesus said to stay dressed for action. Literally the text says let your waist be girded about.

The Freedom of Focus

The irony is that we are bound by truth. That which restricts whatever encumbers us or hampers us actually frees us. Sometimes our mind goes every direction and usually it ends up going somewhere it should not go. We need to restrict our memory, our will, and our affections — as well as our speech. And so this implies discipline. Paul expresses the same thing in 2 Corinthians 10:5, Bring every thought into captivity. Can you see an undisciplined child that someone has to continually chase? They are worn out but have nothing to show for their efforts. A distracted mind can wear us out.

In the context of 1 Peter 1:13 to restrict your mind is related to being *sober*. This word *sober* means to be calm not drunk. It means to be well-balanced, clear headed, self-controlled, restrained, temperate, sober, not confused or governed by emotion.

Then the next phrase then tells us to set our hope on the grace that we will receive when Christ returns. The opposite of a distracted mind is a mind that is set, focused or redirected. How do we maintain a mental attitude of calmness, balance, clear-headed, self control, restrained?

We put a belt around our mind which restrains our thoughts. Nature abhors a vacuum. The way we keep bad thoughts out is to fill our mind with good thoughts. Look at Philippians 4:8. These are the things we are to think about.

- whatever is true
- whatever is honorable
- whatever is just
- whatever is pure
- whatever is lovely
- whatever is commendable

And so the belt is the belt of truth. I'd rather know a few things that are so than a lot of things that are wrong. We are bound by truth and Scripture is the final arbiter of truth.

Look at the context. According to Philippians 4:7 your mind can be at peace, but only if you let that peace guard your mind. The verb *guard* is a military term. In its noun for it is used to describe a sentinel. Eternal vigilance is the price of liberty.

The battle is won or lost in our mind. No soldier is ready for battle if his mind is distracted. Paul wrote in 2 Timothy 2:7 that no soldier gets entangled in civilian pursuits. But in a real sense that which restricts us also frees us. My boundaries become my freedom. The paradox is that the belt frees us.

The Freedom of Order

The belt helps us focus, it pulls in our thoughts. And it helps us organize. Think of a carpenter's belt: hammer, nails, tape measure. An army belt might hold shells, a gun holster, and a canteen.

In those days the belt was also put on first because the sword hung on it and the breastplate rested on it. It was foundational. It helped get organized; it enabled them to get their act together. This is the security of structure.

You will not win the fight because of your belt, but you are not ready to fight until you have tucked in everything that can trip you up and have your weapons in place. Imagine rushing into battle still trying to buckle your belt. When you reach for your sword, you realize it isn't there!

And so this implies organizational management. It's not how hard you work, but how smart you work. What if you work all day on the wrong assignment? We can lose battles because we are in disarray. Most of us need to simplify our lives. You always have time for what you put first. Those who fail to plan, plan to fail. If you aim at nothing you will always hit it!

Metaphorically, this belt helps us set priorities. It helps us pull ourselves together. We need to clarify. We need to delegate. We need to prune.

For Discussion

When seatbelts were first made mandatary, some people resented them as a violation of their personal liberty. However, a seatbelt functions much like this belt does. When a seatbelt is used properly the person who is restrained has been freed from breaking his or her neck!

How does a lion tamer control a lion? I am told that he puts a chair with four legs in the lion's face. Rather than attack the lion freezes because he does not know which leg to attack. I don't know if this is actually true. Try it and let me know if it doesn't work!

The devil know how to act like a lion according to 1 Peter 5:8. But he also knows the trick of a lion tamer!

According to 2 Timothy 2:4 a soldier does not get entangled in civilian pursuits. But in the history of the American revolution there were "summer soldiers and sunshine patriots." Farmers cannot plow straight if they are looking back (Luke 9:62). Discuss how the concept of a belt is both restrictive and liberating.

Discuss how we need to gird our minds. John Wesley said, "I dare no more *fret* than *curse* or *swear*."[7]

> If a dinner ill dressed, a hard bed, a poor room, a shower of rain, or a dusty road, will put them [his traveling companions] out of humor, it lays a burden upon me greater than all the rest put together. By the grace of God I never fret; I repine at nothing; I am discontented with nothing. . . . The doctrine of particular providence is what exceeding few persons understand, at least not practically, so as to apply it

---

[7]Tyerman, *Life and Times of Wesley*, 3:658.

> to every circumstance of life. This I want — to see God acting in everything and disposing all for his own glory and his creatures' good.[8]

Wesley also observed that thanksgiving is "the surest mark of a soul free from anxiety."[9]

---

[8]Wesley, *Letter* to Ebenezer Blackwell, 31 August 1755.

[9]Wesley, *Notes*, 513.

The Protection of a Vest
Ephesians 6:14

Stand therefore having put on the breastplate θώραξ (*thorax*) of righteousness. Today this would be a bullet-proof vest. In those days it was tough leather or metal from the neck to the abdomen to cover our vital organs. But a bullet-proof vest is worn to save life. This breastplate symbolizes emotional protection.

In Jewish thinking the heart was the seat of emotions and feelings. The ancients did not know what we know about psychology. Because they felt a sensation in their organs when they were upset they thought their emotions originated there. Around 400 BC, Hippocrates proposed the theory of four temperaments based on four bodily fluids: blood, phlegm, yellow bile, and black bile — all of which must be kept in balance in order to be in good humor. While this is not accurate scientifically, the important concept for us is that these fluids or humors were thought to originate in the gut organs. Biblical writers reflect this concept.[10] For example

- In the KJV of Psalm 73:21 the word *reins* refers to the kidneys. Modern translations say *mind.*
- In Lamentations 2:11 the KJV refers to the bowels included the liver. The ESV says "my stomach churns," but literally the Hebrew word is *liver.*

We can be hit emotionally so hard that we can't get our breath, our heart pounds, we have panic attacks, our stomach

---

[10]This explanation does not imply that Scripture sanctioned an inaccurate view of psychology. Rather, it records the phenomenal language utilized by the speaker.

tightens, we have indigestion and ulcers, and we cannot sleep. Although we know better we still uses this kind of phenomenal language:

- we say we vent our spleen
- our heart is broken
- our stomach is in knots
- we have butterflies in our stomach

And so Paul is referring to the need to protect our emotions. Proverbs 4:23 teaches us to guard our hearts first because out of the heart flow the issues of life. The direction of our life is set by what flows out of our heart. We cannot stand guard or fight the enemy if we are consumed by our own issues. Too many Christians are overwhelmed with unresolved internal issues.

Our heart is the fountainhead of our life and our life flows out from that source. We need something that protects our emotions, our feelings, our moods. If we do not control anger, bitterness, depression, fear, anxiety, and guilt they will control us and distract us. If you are under emotional stress and strain before you take drugs to escape, make sure you have on the vest of emotional protection. The 1994 edition of the Diagnostic and Statistical Manual of Mental Disorders has three times as many mental disorders listed as the 1952 edition. We have a name for everything and along with it we have an excuse, but not a cure. We need spiritual and emotional healing, but we typically only request prayer for physical illness.

How can this spiritual vest help us emotionally? It is the breastplate of *righteousness*. Here is what Scripture teaches about righteousness:

1. There is none righteous, no not one (Rom 3:10). God alone is righteous (Isa 59:16-17).

2. Religion tends to produce self-righteousness. We are not perfect but better than most. We trust in our good works; we keep the church rules. But we can always do more so religion becomes like a treadmill.

3. God requires us to confess our sins. That is called *repentance*. When we plead guilty and trust in Christ, God forgives us and declares us to be righteous. See Romans 3:21-26; 4:5. Dr. Karl Menninger said that if he could convince his patients in psychiatric hospitals that their sins were forgiven, 75% could walk out the next day!

4. According to Ephesians 4:24 we are to put off the old life and put on the new life, created to be like God in true righteousness and holiness.

> Many, if not most, of the emotional and relational problems Christians experience are caused by lack of personal holiness . . . . the church today is often guilty of supplying believers with the paper armor of good advice, programs, activities, techniques, and methods — when what they need is godly armor of holy living.[11]

5. Those who are righteous live by faith

Satan will accuse us. He knows just which button to push to set us off emotionally. He may come at us through the

---

[11]MacArthur, *Ephesians*, 353.

words of another person. He may remind us of some past sin. We may worry that we are not good enough and other people may not accept us.

Romans 8:31 declares that God is for us, not against us. And if God be for us, who can be against us? Sometimes it feels like everyone is against us! But the point is that we are trying to please God not them. We do not have to get upset, agitated, and fearful. Those who have been justified have peace with God (Rom 5:1). If I know where I stand with God, I can't be controlled by what others say about me.

> Does the enemy bring up against me my old sins? I can say: "It is God that justifieth; who is he that condemneth?" Am I tempted to presume on my forgiveness, and to fall into transgression once more? From this breastplate the arrow of temptation falls pointless, as it resounds: "He that doesth righteousness is righteous. He that is born of God doth not commit sin." The completeness of pardon for past offence and the integrity of character that belong to the justified life are woven together into an impenetrable mail.[12]

But I still feel condemnation. 1 John 3:20 If my heart condemns me God is greater than my heart and he knows everything. So he will convict us specifically of what we did wrong. Then I acknowledge that I was wrong and ask his forgiveness.

But if my heart does not condemn me specifically I stand on my relationship not how I feel. Some people are overly conscientious and are controlled by others. If I have not delib-

---

[12]Findlay, *Ephesians*, 415.

erately or knowingly rebelled against God (v 19), I reassure my heart before him and the false guilt will evaporate. Love will roll the clouds away.

Do I believe God's Word or do I believe my doubts? Don't accept the false condemnation of others or the accusations of Satan. Don't even judge yourself. If you will *stand* on the Word, eventually your feelings will catch up.

For Discussion

John Wesley preached that the religion of Jesus Christ is God's method of healing a diseased soul. "Hereby the great Physician of souls applies medicine to heal *this sickness*; to restore human nature, totally corrupted in all its faculties."

> Know your disease! Know your cure! Ye were born in sin; therefore "ye must be born again," "born of God." By nature ye are wholly corrupted; by grace ye shall be wholly renewed. . . . Now "go on" "from faith to faith," until your whole sickness be healed.[13]

Discuss salvation as spiritual healing. Do you think we would feel better physically if we felt better emotionally? Explore the psychosomatic connection.

In *Healing Grace* by David Seamands, there is a section called "Gut-Level Grace." Get someone to read and report on this section.[14]

The eradication doctrine of the holiness movement teaches that those who are sanctified will not feel certain emotions. However, in Ephesians 4:26 Paul does not command us to put off anger because anger is an involuntary emotion and it is impossible to avoid all provocation. Instead, we are cautioned that anger can easily lead to sin. There is only one letter difference between anger and *d*anger! In v 31 Paul cites six sins of anger that Christians are to get rid of, take away, remove, destroy, or kill. Here are the six sinful expressions of anger which Paul forbids in Ephesians 4:31:

---

[13]Wesley, "Original Sin" Sermon #44, 3.3-5.

[14]Seamands, *Healing Grace*, 27-30

1. **Bitterness**, a bitter jealousy; smouldering resentment about the past. Deal with issues quickly and do not let them simmer lest a bitter root grows up (Heb 12:15).

2. **Wrath** or rage, an uncontrolled anger, explosive temper, or boiling agitation. This includes invoking a curse upon our enemies, swearing to hurt them, or using crude and offensive language which is abusive and demeaning.

3. **Anger**, a gnawing hostility or a settled feeling of hatred. This is the third use of some form of this word in this section. The verb form is used in v 26 and there anger is allowed but it is to be resolved quickly. Here it is a noun and represents a condition that has not been settled. In 5:6 it is used of God's wrath. Some personality types hold it all in until they burst and go on a rampage.

4. **Clamor** brawling, angry yelling or outcry.

5. **Evil speaking** or slander, which is the abuse and accusation of others. It is *blasphemy* when God is slandered; *abusive* language when to others. Be slow to jump to conclusion, assign motives, or pass judgment.

6. **Malice** literally is *evil*, a generic term meaning any attitude or action which intends harm to your neighbor. Since the context of this verse has been unacceptable forms of speech, this refers in context to an intention to bring harm through what we say. It is an attitude of vindictiveness.

Process how the vest of emotional protection can keep us from spiritual "infection" when we have been provoked.

Amanda Smith (1837–1915), a renowned 19th-century American Methodist evangelist and former slave, said "When a cloud comes over your soul, look to see if sin has caused the darkness, and if not, go right on setting the table for the Lord." Discuss how this applies to the breastplate.

Should we ever let our guard down? Under what conditions? In order to protect our emotions there are times in which we have to establish boundaries with people who are controlling, manipulative, and accusing.

The Mobility of the Sure-Footed
Ephesians 6:15

The verb *shod* or *fitted* means to bind under or to put sandals under our feet. This results in ἑτοιμασία (*hetoimasia*) or readiness. Peace with God and mankind makes us sure-footed. We cannot go into battle barefooted! And so the church is the equipment room — the footlocker — where we are outfitted for battle.

Sandals were not usually worn indoors in Bible times. The wealthy had servants who carried their sandals for them. When they were needed the servant tied them on their feet and when they were not needed, the servant loosened them. However, the warrior was not ready for action until his sandals were tightly fastened.

Both Julius Caesar and Alexander the Great were successful because they could march their troops over long distances quickly — often over rough terrain — and thus catch the enemy unprepared. They learned to put studs or nails on the sole so that they did not slip.

Proper shoes are still important. Nothing will help you forget all of your other problems like tight shoes! A former member told me that when he was inducted into the military they threw his uniform to him, but spent 1½ hours fitting his shoes. Like many veterans, he no longer fits in his uniform, but he can still wear those shoes.

- Habakkuk 3:19
- Psalm 18:33
- 2 Samuel 22:34

— all describe the grace of deer who are sure-footed on high mountainous terrain. Some of us are not are graceful! And so

Paul's message to us is — don't let the devil trip you up. If we don't watch him he will tie our shoestrings together and we get so tangled up that we fall down. Ralph Earle explained, "God's peace gives us firm footing in fighting the enemy."[15]

- Jude 1:24 declares that he is able to keep us from stumbling.
- Psalm 94:18 assures us that when we slip, he will hold us up.
- Psalm 37:23-24 says

  The LORD makes firm the steps of the one who delights in him; though he may stumble, he will not fall, for the LORD upholds him with his hand. NIV

  How do we become sure-footed?

- Are you at peace with God? Romans 5:1

- Are you at peace with yourself? According to Philippians 4:7-9 we guard our minds. Thus, when our peace of mind is breached we look to see why. This is our Early Warning Defense System.

- Does peace rule in your relationships? Colossians 3:15 describes peace as an arbitrator or umpire.

Ephesians 4:3 refers to the bond of peace. This implies that peace has a unifying effect; it fastens us together. In the fourth century Chrysostom preached,

---

[15]Earle, *Word Meanings*, 4:348.

> Bind yourself to your brethren. Those thus bound together in love bear everything with ease. . . . Beautiful is this bond. With this bond we bind ourselves together both to one another and to God.[16]

Therefore, Hebrews 12:14 commands us to pursue peace with everyone although Romans 12:18 concedes that may not always be possible.

- This mobility equips us to spread the peace of the gospel. See Isaiah 52:7. The paradox is that we fight the spiritual battle by spreading peace — unlike the Quran doctrine of jihad. The weapons of our warfare are not carnal (2 Cor 10:4).

But we must have peace before we spread it. Thus we kill them with kindness. Or better put, we destroy our enemies by leading them to Christ. Then they are our brothers and sisters in the faith.

> Attack is often the best mode of defense. We keep our faith by spreading it. We defend ourselves from our opponents by converting them to the gospel.[17]

---

[16]Edwards, *ACCS*, 8:159.

[17]Findlay, *Ephesians*, 417.

For Discussion

If I was your basketball coach my final words to you in the locker room would be — check your shoes. Are you ready? Whether we are talking about basketball shoes or combat boots — you are not ready until you have your shoes on.

What does it mean to say that we cannot fight externally until we have victory internally? How does the devil use unresolved internal conflict to trip us up or ties us in knots? To use another popular idiom — how do we shoot ourselves in the foot?

Do you like this term — we kill our enemies with kindness? It is based on Romans 12:18-21. Augustine said that the coals of fire heaped upon our enemies head are the burning pangs of shame or anguish which lead to repentance (v 20; see Prov 25:21-22).[18]

In early Methodist history the story is told that Thomas Reader became so angry at John Fletcher's *Last Check to Antinomianism* that he traveled all the way to Madeley to rebuke the author. Upon his arrival, Fletcher exclaimed, "Come in, come in, thou blessed of the Lord! Am I so honored as to receive a visit from so esteemed a servant of my Master? Let us have a little prayer, while refreshments are getting ready." Reader reported that he never so enjoyed three days of such spiritual and profitable conversation in all his life, but was never able to muster enough courage to even allude to the purpose of his visit.[19]

In historical context, Thomas Reader was a zealous Cal-

---

[18]*Bray*, *ACCS*, 6:322.

[19]Tyerman, *Wesley's Designated Successor*, 320-321.

vinist and Fletcher's book was defending the possibility of deliverance from sin in this life. Truth matters, but we must speak the truth in love (Eph 4:15). Some people are too "loving" to offend the devil and their counterparts have zeal without wisdom (or love). They epitomize the observation, "Fools rush in where angels fear to tread."

Sometimes Christians are as mean-spirited as those who do not profess any grace. We prepare ourselves for battle by first getting right with God. Then we win the battle by letting God work through us. There may be various approaches to evangelism, but the bottom line is that we catch more flies with honey than with vinegar. Is it possible to be tough *and* tender?

How many times have you rushed into battle, only to trip up on your own shoelaces? Instead of defending truth and proclaiming Jesus, you ended up reaching to personal insult and accusations that revealed your own unresolved issues and insecurities.

If a picture is worth a thousand words, draw this cartoon:

- the house is engulfed in flames
- only one straggler lags inside
- the fire chief gives his final warning over a bull-horn
- the straggler responds that he will be out in seconds — he only needs to put his shoes on
- the shoes are nowhere to be found or separated or tied together in knots

Compare girding up your loins and tightening up your sandals. In both cases the point is that there is freedom in restriction. In one case the flowing robes are an obvious impediment, but improperly tied sandals may not be as obvious cause of stumbling.

The Covering of Faith
Ephesians 6:16

This shield was about four feet high and 2½ feet wide. It was like a door with an iron frame. It was made of wood, it was curved, and covered with leather or metal. If leather was used, it would be soaked in water before battle.[20] It was called a *scutum*.

The phrase ἐν πᾶσιν (*en pasin*) means besides all — after you have girded up your loins, positioned the breastplate, and tied up your sandals, *then* you pick up this shield. The shield is not more important than the rest of the armor — we must wear it all. However, the shield requires one hand to hold and you must put on these other pieces first.

We need cover because we are under attack. The devil schemes (v 11) and he has levels of minions under his authority (v 12). One of their methods is to shoot flaming arrows at us. This was an ancient method of warfare. They dipped the tip of the dart or arrow in pitch and lit it. It would burn brightly as it sped through the air and wherever it landed it would start a fire. In early American history the Indians did this, setting fire to houses and settlements. The arrows shot at us are flaming arrows of temptation that inflame us to sin. Wesley described Satan's darts as "his evil suggestions of every kind, blasphemous or unclean."[21]

For example, Proverbs 6-7 warns against adultery. Notice how this temptation is connected with fire. When a man is seduced, this is described as being pierced by an arrow (Prov 7:23). Can a man scoop fire into his lap without his clothes

---

[20]Brown, "War," 3:966.

[21]Wesley, "Of Evil Angels," Sermon #72, 3.1.

being burned? Can a man walk on hot coals without his feet being scorched? So is he who sleeps with another man's wife (Prov 6:27-29).

Another example is gossip. "Their tongue is a deadly arrow; it speaks with deceit. With his mouth each speaks cordially to his neighbor, but in his heart he sets a trap for him" (Jer 9:8). According to James, "The tongue also is a fire, a world of evil among the parts of the body. It corrupts the whole person, sets the whole course of his life on fire, and is itself set on fire by hell (Jas 3:6). So the devil tempts us through inflammatory suggestions and words.

Through faith we have adequate protection. The shield had a second function. It was also used as a stretcher to carry the wounded from the battlefield. As their sons left for battle, Greek mothers gave them their shield and told them, "My son, with this or upon it."[22] But when we are under attack, faith can defuse every temptation. Through faith we can extinguish *all* temptation. The *all* promises that we need not ever become casualties.

E. M. Bounds, "No battle was ever planned by hell's most gifted strategist which can conquer faith. All its inflamed and terrible darts fall harmless as they strike against the shield of faith."[23]

> The evil thoughts which he suggests are like *burning darts*: for they tend to kindle strange fire in the hearts of men. But they cannot injure those "guarded in the power of God through *faith* (1 Peter 1:5). Since faith is thus a complete protection, it is here

---

[22]Carter, *Wesleyan Bible Commentary*, 5:439.

[23]Bounds, *Satan*, 152.

> called a *shield able to quench all the burning darts* cast against it. Paul thus teaches the absolute safety of those who believe.[24]

> Faith makes the devil tremble; it drives him away; he is a mere coward, when he grapples with a man that has the shield of faith; he flies away; the word of faith wounds his head, retorts all his darts upon himself, and make him bite his chains.[25]

But we must grasp how faith works. Too often people who have never submitted to God's will and are living in willful sin, carelessly and prayerlessly get into trouble and think faith is saying the magic words "I believe" and God is obligated to bail them out like a "Get Out of Jail Free" card in Monopoly.

Shield of faith means the shield which consists of faith. Grammatically this is a genitive of apposition where a noun in the genitive case defines, explains, or provides a specific example of a preceding noun. It is best translated by replacing *of* with *namely* or *which is*. So what is faith? How does it protect me?

- Faith must have a foundation or adequate basis. It means to trust the Word of God which is based on the nature of God. According to Psalm 138:2 there is no division between who God is and what he says. We must know who God is and trust his character (Heb 11:6).

---

[24]Beet, *Ephesians*, 373.

[25]Walsh, "The Whole Armor of God," 227.

- *Believe* means we must act on what we know to be true. Faith is trusting God's Word. True faith always leads to action.

If you have been careless, bring yourself to attention. If you have sinned, acknowledge it and repent. Humble yourself and submit to God. Tighten up your belt, tie your shoes, pick up your breastplate of righteousness.

> Submit yourselves to God. Resist the devil and he will flee from you. Come near to God and he will come near to you. Wash your hands, you sinners, and purify your hearts, you double-minded. Grieve, mourn and wail. Change your laughter to mourning and your joy to gloom. Humble yourselves before the Lord and he will lift you up (Jas 4:7-10).

This is all the obedience of faith (Rom 1:5, 16:26). As we actively trust in God, and submit to him, the devil will flee. "Faith takes hold of God's resources in the midst of the onslaught of evil and produces the firm resolve which douses anything the enemy throws at the believer."[26]

Adam Clarke explained,

> He who walks so as to feel the witness of God's Spirit that he is his child, as all evil thoughts in abhorrence; and, though they pass through his mind, they never fix in his passions. They are caught on this shield, blunted, and extinguished.[27]

---

[26]Lincoln, *WBC*, 42:449.

[27]Clarke, *Commentary*, 6:471.

Here Clarke echos the famous statement by Martin Luther, You cannot keep birds from flying over your head but you can keep them from building a nest in your hair.[28] The hymn “I Need Thee Every Hour” says “temptations lose their power, when thou art nigh.”

Wesley preached,

> The more you are tempted to give up your shield, to cast away your faith, your confidence in his love, so much the more take heed that you hold fast that whereunto you have attained. So much the more labor to “stir up the gift of God which is in you.”[29]

Faith also has a corporate aspect. Ancient armies marched with shields side by side. They could form a front line a mile or so long. Archers shot at the enemy behind this wall of shields. We need the protection of each other. I may need to stop and retie my sandal. My little shield affords me only about 2½ feet of cover, if I stand alone. But if I stand in solidarity with other believers I could have a covering that spanned a mile or more!

The church should be an unbroken wall. It is weakened where there is a gap. If I am AWOL my brother or sister may be left vulnerable. It takes full compliment of teeth to eat corn on the cob, not merely a straggling tooth here and there.

We stand in solidarity for the faith which was once for all delivered (Jude 3) but which we must personally trust. That is why we recite the creeds corporately. That is the corporate expression of our faith. Here we are looking at *faith* as a

---

[28]Luther, *Exposition on the Lord's Prayer*, 89.

[29]Wesley, “Satan's Devices,” Sermon #42, 2.3.

noun, not a verb. Creeds are affirmations of *the faith*. We also act on that faith as we trust and obey. If you are in the devil's cross-hairs, get behind the protection of the church and find someone to whom you can be accountable.

If I keep the faith when I am living, the faith will keep me when I am dying *and* when I am under attack.

For Discussion

See Psalm 7:10-16 where God comes after the defiant person and shoots him down with flaming arrows. Discuss this reverse picture. God will either fight for us or fight against us.

The best commentary on the shield of faith is found in *Pilgrim's Progress* in the conflict between Christian and Apollyon. John Bunyan wrote that Apollyon had been reminding Christian of his infirmities. Then Apollyon attacked him by throwing a flaming dart at his breast which he intended to kill Christians. "But Christian held a shield in his hand, with which he caught it, and so prevented the danger of that."

In Ezekiel 22:30 God is described as seeking for someone to fill the hole, plug the hole, or stand in the breach. Could that be where you fit? Edward Everett Hale is famous for the statement,

> I am only one, but I am one. I cannot do everything, but I can do something. And because I cannot do everything, I will not refuse to do the something that I can do.

Discuss how a healthy church is a shelter for the wounded and how a toxic church shoots its wounded.

Getting Your Head Straight
Ephesians 6:17

Even with a shield, the soldier's head would frequently rise above it. The word *helmet* simply means around the head. It was made of bronze. It was adorned with emblems on its crest or ridge. As Paul looked at his Romans guards he gave us this command to take, receive, or accept the helmet which is salvation. *Salvation* (σωτήριος - *soterios*) is a broad word meaning protection, deliverance, and preservation.

Just as the breastplate protected those vital organs which were considered the center of our emotions, so the head is where our brain is located. Thus, this helmet protects our mind. The mind is where most battles are fought. We must take control of our mind and arrest every thought that is contrary to the word of God (2 Cor 10:4-5). We may be born again in a moment of time, but we may spend a lifetime learning to think like a Christian.

We need to be protected from deception, doubt, and despair.

1. The discipline of truth

THE FIVE BIGGEST LIES SATAN EVER TOLD

1. That he is coequal with God. This is dualism.
2. God's Word is not trustworthy and we are the final authority. This is humanism.
3. There is no God. This is atheism.
4. Salvation does not deliver from sin. Hence, sin is sovereign.
5. Christ's kingdom will fail. Hence, Satan will win.

2. The discipline of faith

I refuse to doubt God. Growing up my pastor said that some people doubted their faith and believed their doubts. We need to affirm our faith and reject our doubts. Every Sunday we affirm "I believe" when we recite the Apostles' Creed. Augustine said, "Therefore do not seek to understand in order to believe, but believe that thou mayest understand."[30]

Faith is a powerful weapon against Satan. "For everyone born of God overcomes the world. This is the victory that has overcome the world, even our faith. Who is it that overcomes the world? Only the one who believes that Jesus is the Son of God" (1 John 5:4-5).

We cannot trust and fear at the same time. Fear does not come from God. "For God gave us a spirit not of fear but of power and love and self-control" (2 Tim 1:7). The KJV said "sound mind." This Greek word means self-controlled and sensible. The root word is *phren* from which we get diaphragm. The ancients regarded the diaphragm as the seat of the mind and of the emotions. Thus, it was described as a fence or hedge around the mind and emotions. The term σωφρονισμός (*sophronismos*) is a compound word — *saved* + *phren*.

While we know today that the diaphragm is not the actual center of emotional balance, we are aware that it is effected when we are off balance emotionally. It controls our breathing, keeping us level. God can keep you level-headed, but fear will cause panic and overreaction, hyperventilation and having our wind knocked out of us.

---

[30]Augustine, *Homilies on the Gospels*. Tractate 29 on John 7:14-18. *NPNF*1 7:184.

3. The discipline of hope

First Thessalonians 5:8 tells us to put on the hope of salvation as a helmet. Paul describes the Christian's emblem as hope. Clarke wrote,

> The *hope* of continual safety and protection, built on the promises of God, to which the upright followers of Christ feels he has a Divine right, protects the *understanding* from being darkened, and the judgment from being confused by any temptations of Satan, or subtle arguments of the sophistical ungodly.[31]

Wesley counseled, "If he inject doubts whether you are a child of God, or fears lest you should not endure to the end, "Take to you for a helmet, the hope of salvation."[32]

But sinners are without hope (Eph 2:2). While they may say they hope something good will happen, that is only wishful thinking. According to Rom 5:5 Christian hope never disappoints.

> Biblical hope is inseperable therefore from faith in God. Because of what God has done in the past, particularly in preparing for the coming of Christ, and because of what God has done and is now doing through Christ, the Christian dares to expect future blessings at present invisible.[33]

---

[31]Clarke, *Commentary*, 6:471.

[32]Wesley, "Of Evil Angels," Sermon #72, 3.3.

[33]Tasker, "Hope," 489.

The Greek word for *hope* carries the idea of expectation or confidence. Hope is faith for the future. Paul prayed in Eph 1:18 that Christians might know the hope to which God has called us. Love always hopes (1 Cor 13:7).

Have you lost hope? It is a tactic of the devil to convince us things are hopeless. We must reprogram our minds. Don't lose hope.

- hope is the anchor of the soul - Heb 6:19

> So hope keeps the soul calm and steadfast, in the midst of temptations and persecutions; it looks for good things to come.[34]

- We are saved by hope - Rom 8:24.
- Love always hopes - 1 Cor 13:7

> Hope, as a helmet covers his head; it lifts him up when he is ready to sink. When the devil and the world, beat on the head of the righteous, their helmet defends them; for hope is patient, and patience overcomes all difficulties.[35]

---

[34]Walsh, "The Whole Armor of God," 228.

[35]Walsh, "The Whole Armor of God," 229.

For Discussion

A. W. Tozer wrote *I Talk Back to the Devil* (1972). Tozer said that the devil attempts to intimidate, magnifies memories, and paralyze through the fear of fanaticism. He does not advocate berating the devil, as described in Jude 9. Rather, he advocates that we push back and resist the devil (Jas 4:7) by learning to think biblically. Reflect on how the devil tries to get into your head.

Discuss the five biggest lies that Satan has ever told? Do you agree? What lies has he told you?

Learning to Handle the Sword
Ephesians 6:17

After we are covered, we attack. This sword is the only offensive weapon.

1. Our sword is God's Word

Jesus had a high view of Scripture. He said every word came from the mouth of God (Matt 4:4). In Revelation 1:16 Jesus is described as having a sharp, two-edged sword coming from his mouth. This is repeated in 2:12. In 19:15-21 Jesus rides the white horse, a sharp sword comes from his mouth. It has authority to rule the nations. In v 21 it slays the kings of the earth.

- It is big. The Greek word ῥομφαία (*rhomphaia*) describes a 3-4 feet long and took both hands to wield.

- We are told it comes from God's mouth. This illustrates 2 Timothy 3:16 that it is God-breathed. That is his inspiration. What comes from God contains no error. See Psalm 138:2

- It is sharp. Not dull. Sharp things have a point! It is living. It has energy. J. B. Phillips paraphrased the New Testament in sections from 1947-1957. As he handled God's Word he said he felt rather like an electrician rewiring an ancient house without being able to turn the mains off.[36]

-

---

[36]Phillips, *Letters to Young Churches*, xi.

- It is two-edged. See Hebrews 4:12. It cuts both ways. It contains both promise and judgment. Those who rebel come under judgment; those who submit to the knife find healing. See this described in Deuteronomy 32:39.

2. Our sword will defeat Satan

Jesus used it in Matthew 4. After fasting forty days and nights, he was weakened with hunger. Satan tried three lines of temptation. In each attack Jesus responded, *It is written*. This verb is in the perfect tense - its stand written. In each instance he quoted from Deuteronomy. E. M. Bounds wrote,

> We cannot make too much of the Word of God. Christ foiled Satan with it. If we be valiant, true, and invincible, we also must have the Word of God dwelling in us richly . . . As a weapon of defense and offense, God has magnified His Word above all His name. Thrice armed against all Satan's wiles and his devices, are those who are filled with God's Word.[37]

Submit yourselves, then to God. Resist the devil and he will flee from you. Draw near to God and he will draw near to you. Humble yourselves before the Lord, and he will life you up (Jas 4:7-10).

3. We must learn how to handle properly (2 Tim 2:15).

Some people put a statue on their dashboard. Another religion brings their converts to the temple and gives them magic underwear to protect them against the devil. Most

---

[37]Bounds, *Satan*, 153-154.

people file their important papers in the big family Bible on the coffee table that gathers dust!

You cannot use the Word effectively until you have personally submitted to its authority. The believer cannot exercise authority until he has come under authority.

The centurion in Matthew 8:8-9 understood the principle of authority because he was a man *under* authority (v 9). Then he proceeds to describe his authority. Those under him do what he says. He has authority *over* a hundred men. He realizes that he has authority *over* a realm only so long as he is *under* authority. In medieval times when a person was knighted the sword was dubbed on their shoulder, then strapped to their side. We come under this authority before we wield it.

You master the Word by living it. The way to get a good grip on this sword is to allow it to control your thinking. Often people are intimidated by the word *theology*. But everyone is a theologian. Everyone has some concept of God. The only question is whether your theology is adequate.

In the Greek New Testament two words are used for sword. I have already described the big sword. But *machaira* is a short sword or dagger, 6-18 inches long. If you keep downloading the whole book, the Holy Spirit can pull up just the right verse you need in your battle. It is the work of the Holy Spirit to bring the Word to our remembrance (John 14:26). Adam Clarke,

> An ability to quote this on proper occasions, and especially in times of temptation and trial, has a wonderful tendency to cut in pieces the snares of the adversary. In God's word a genuine Christian may have unlimited confidence, and to every purpose to which it is applicable it may be brought with the

greatest effect.[38]

Is your sword rusty, dull, dusty? Man does not live by bread alone, but by every word that comes from the mouth of God (Matt 4:4).

For Discussion

God's Word is the only weapon we need. He need not return to conquer the nations. His authority is not restricted to his location. His Word subdues the nations. He does not return to rescue a defeated church, but instead he remains at the Father's right hand in heaven until every enemy has been defeated (Ps 110:1). Process this concept of victory and our role in preaching the Word.

---

[38]Clarke, *Commentary*, 6:471.

The Preparation of Prayer
Ephesians 6:18-20

Paul uses the word *all* four times in v 18. Regardless of the English translation some form of the Greek adjective πᾶς (*pas*) occurs four times:

- the variety of prayer. We are to pray *all* kinds of prayer.
- the frequency of prayer. We are to pray on *all* occasions.
- the intensity of prayer. We are to pray *always*.
- the objects of prayer. We are to pray for *all* the saints.

In v 18 Paul begins with a general verb for prayer — προσεύχομαι (*proseuchomai*). We are to pray in the Spirit. This is described in Romans 8:26-27. Prayer is nothing else but the soul speaking to God. It is the very breath of faith. Therefore it is as natural to a real Christian as to breathe.[39] You cannot stand fast in the faith, or grow in grace, unless you continue instant in prayer.[40]

Paul continues with

- προσευχή (*proseuche*) - the noun form of the verb also used in v 18
- request or petition (δέησις - *deesis*) heart-felt petition arising from deep personal need.
- then he says be alert. This verb ἀγρυπνέω (*agrupneo*) is a military term but he is still talking about prayer. Jesus told his disciples to "watch and pray so that you will not enter into temptation" (Matt 26:41).
- *Deesis* is used again in v 18. Paul continues by saying we

---

[39] Walsh, "The Whole Armor of God," 232.

[40] Walsh, "The Whole Armor of God," 239.

are to make supplication for all the saints — including him.

There are four synonyms for prayer used in 2 Timothy 2:1. After considering a total of seven words for prayer, Trench concluded that they do not set forth different kinds of prayer, but prayer contemplated from different sides and under different aspects.[41]

We will find ourselves in spiritual battle whether or not we have prayed, but if we are not prayed up we are not ready to fight. Through prayer we are alerted to danger (v 11). How can we watch out for an invisible enemy? Through prayer the Holy Spirit can help us discern the enemy's strategy. In Ephesians 1:18 Paul prays that the eyes of our heart might be enlightened. Through prayer we can see some things more clearly with our eyes closed! Prayer moves the hand of God. Wesley said that God does nothing but in answer to prayer.[42]

Literally the text says that we are to pray *at every time*. Do you want an anti-ballistic missle system that works every other day? Have you seen this sign? "This property protected by a pit bull two days per week — you guess which two?" But what if the devil knows which two days per week you pray?

Prayer must be consistent. We cannot continually be engaged in formal prayer, but we should pray consistently about all things.

Paul also addresses the intensity of prayer. We ask more than once.

The "perseverance" he requires in this wakeful

---

[41]Trench, *Synonyms*, 192.

[42]Wesley, *BE Works*, 13:127.

> attention to prayer, is the resolute persistence of the supplicant, who will neither be daunted by opposition nor wearied by delay.[43]

Paul even specifies the objects of prayer. We are to pray for *all* the saints. Prayer must be unselfish. Wesley observed, "Perhaps we receive few answers to prayer, because we do not intercede enough for others."[44]

Prayer is the most powerful weapon we have. Yes, prayer is a weapon but it is not symbolized as a weapon in this context. Whether we count prayer as the seventh piece of armor or whether we "put on the gospel armor, each piece put on with prayer,"[45] is an interpretative issue. However, it does not make too much difference practically.[46]

> This great requirement of standing ready for the combat can be made good only when prayer, constant, earnest, spiritual prayer, is added to the careful equipment with all the parts of the panoply.[47]

---

[43]Findlay, *Ephesians*, 423.

[44]Wesley, *Notes*, 503.

[45]George Duffield, Jr. "Stand Up, Stand Up for Jesus" (1858).

[46]Verses 14-20 constitute one sentence. The main verb *stand* in v 14 is followed by seven aorist participles: having fastened on the belt, having put on the breastplate, having put on shoes, taking up the shield and the helmet, taking the sword, praying and keeping alert. Grammatically being alert is just as much a participle as prayer. Since neither alert nor prayer is symbolized it does not seem that Paul intended to include them as armor.

[47]Salmond, "*Ephesians*," 389. *Panoply* means the complete set of armor. It occurs in Luke 11:22; Eph 6:11, and 13.

"Without this, a man can neither obtain, nor preserve any part of the Divine armor."[48]

Having done all *stand*. But do not stand in the confidence that we have done all we can do. We stand in the finished work of Christ. We stand on his continual intercession (Heb 7:25). Watchman Nee outlined the book of Ephesians based on the postures of the Christian. We sit with Christ (Eph 2:6). We walk worthy of our calling (Eph 4:1). And we stand against the devil (Eph 6:11).

Prayer is standing before God's mirror. Are you covered? How do you dress for battle? Put on each piece prayerfully:

Are you distracted? Put on your belt.
Are you vulnerable? Put on your vest.
Are you unprepared? Tie your shoes.
Are you covered? Pick up your shield.
Are you deceived? Put on your helmet.
Are you disarmed? Pick up your sword.

---

[48]Walsh, "The Whole Armor of God," 231.

For Discussion

The March 1996 issue of *Reader's Digest* contained an article on the power of prayer. It claimed, "Scientists are discovering what believers have always known." Is it necessary for prayer to be validated scientifically? How would science go about "proving" this claim?

There is a famous line from Alfred, Lord Tennyson's poem, "Morte d'Arthur," "More things are wrought by prayer than this world dreams of." How would science count every such answer to prayer?

Human personality is comprised of intellect, will, and emotions. In order to be fully protected we need to cover our mind. Discuss which piece of armor symbolically covers our mind.

As soldiers, we are not "at ease." We must be on guard. Which pieces of armor symbolize intentionality? And which piece of armor symbolically protects our emotions?

Prayer may start with me and my needs, but it should not end with me. What do you think of John Wesley's reflection, "Perhaps we receive few answers to prayer, because we do not intercede enough for others"?

Standing Your Ground

Currently some 23 states have a version of "Stand Your Ground" laws. Such laws permit individuals to use reasonable, including deadly, force in self-defense without a duty to retreat from a threat if they are in a place they have a legal right to be.

How can we aggressively advance the kingdom? There is nothing which requires more effort than intercessory prayer, which includes fasting, carrying a burden, wrestling, and spiritual warfare. Praying is the hardest thing we can do. Martin Luther said, "Prayer is indeed a continuous violent action of the spirit as it is lifted up to God. This action is comparable to that of a ship going against the stream."[49] Samuel Chadwick wrote,

> Intensity is a law of prayer. God is found by those who seek Him with all their heart. Wrestling prayer prevails. The fervent, effectual prayer of the righteous is a great force.[50]

Fervency is a sanctified determination. John Fletcher wrote,

> The grand device of Satan is to prevent us from seeing the necessity of this holy violence, or from putting it in execution. . . . A humble, holy, sacred violence must be used in prayer — with Jesus, that he would open in our hearts the power of faith, apply

---

[49]Bloesch, *The Struggle of Prayer*, 132.

[50]Chadwick, *The Path of Prayer*, 49.

> the efficacy of his blood, and bestow upon us the spirit of prayer; or in other words the prayer of faith, — with the Father, that he would look through the pillar of fire, and discomfit all our enemies, — with the Holy Ghost, that he would take up his abode with us.[51]

May we not rest nor give God any rest until he establishes Jerusalem (Isa 62:6-7). Wesley explained that *Zion* and *Jerusalem* were terms used for the church, according to Hebrews 12:22.[52] God's covenant people should be consumed with zeal for God's house. Under the old covenant, his house was his temple, the place where he dwells. Today the whole world is his temple and filled with his glory (Isa 6:3). Therefore, we should be zealous to see his kingdom agenda advanced. David declared that zeal for God's house consumed him (Ps 69:9). This passion characterized Jesus (John 2:17) and should characterize his people. We should seek first his kingdom (Matt 6:33). We should always give ourselves fully to the work of the Lord (1 Cor 15:58).

Joseph Sutcliffe wrote, "He who besieges the throne of grace by faith and prayer, is sure to prevail."[53] In Luke 12:49-53 Jesus taught that we will undergo a baptism of fire to set up his kingdom. Once in that kingdom we will not experience universal peace but rather the fiery trial of war. Let us pray for revival and the advancement of God's kingdom and take it by storm.

---

[51]Fletcher, *Works*, 4:261-262.

[52]Wesley, *Notes*, 3:2109.

[53]Sutcliffe, *Commentary*, IIA:67.

BIBLIOGRAPHY

Augustine. *Homilies on the Gospels. A Select Library of the Nicene and Post-Nicene Fathers of the Christian Church.* First Series. Vol. 6. Philip Schaff, ed. 1887. Reprint, Grand Rapids: Eerdmans, 1979. [*NPNF*]

Beet, Joseph Agar. *A Commentary on St. Paul's Epistles to the Ephesians, Philippians, Colossians, and to Philemon.* 1890. Reprint, Salem, OH; Schmul 1994.

Bloesch, Donald G. *The Struggle of Prayer.* San Francisco: Harper & Row, 1980.

Bray, Gerald. *Romans: Ancient Christian Commentary on Scripture.* Thomas C. Oden, ed. Downers Grove, IL: InterVarsity, 1998. [*ACCS*]

Brown, Colin. "War." *The New International Dictionary of New Testament Theology.* Grand Rapids: Zondervan, 1976. 3:958-967.

Bounds, E. M. *Satan: His Personality, Power and Overthrow.* 1922. Reprint, Grand Rapids: Baker, 1972.

Carter, Charles W. "1 Corinthians and Ephesians." *The Wesleyan Bible Commentary.* 7 vol. Grand Rapids: Baker, 1966.

Calvin, John. *Commentaries on the Epistles of Paul to the Galatians and Ephesians.* 1548. Translated by William Prigle. Reprinted, Grand Rapids: Baker, 1979.

Chadwick, Samuel. *The Path of Prayer.* London: Hodder &

Stoughton, 1931.
Clarke, Adam. *The Holy Bible, Containing the Old and New Testaments: The Text Carefully Printed from the Most Correct Copies of the Present Authorized Translations, Including the Marginal reading and Parallel Texts; with a Commentary and Critical Notes, Designed as a help to a Better Understanding of the Sacred Writings*. 6 vols. 1811-1825. Reprinted, Nashville, Abingdon, 1950.
Earle, Ralph. *Word Meanings in the New Testament*. 6 vols. Kansas City: Beacon Hill, 1979.
Edwards, Mark J. Galatians, *Ephesians, Philippians: Ancient Christian Commentary on Scripture*. Thomas C. Oden, ed. Downers Grove, IL: InterVarsity, 1999. [*ACCS*]
Findlay, George G. *The Epistle to the Ephesians. The Expositor's Bible*. 3rd ed. W. Robertson Nicoll, ed. New York: A. C. Armstrong and Son, 1898. First edition 1892.
Fletcher, John. *The Works of the Reverend John Fletcher*. 4 vols. 1833. Reprinted, Salem, OH: Schmul, 1974.
Hanegraff, Hank. *The Covering*. Nashville: Thomas Nelson, 2002.
Lewis, C. S. *The Screwtape Letters*. New York: Macmillan, 1943.
Lincoln, Andrew T. *Ephesians: Word Biblical Commentary*. Vol 42. Dallas: Word, 1990.
Luther, Martin. *Exposition of the Lord's Prayer*. Thomas Nunn, transl. London: James Nisbit, 1844.
MacArthur, John. *The MacArthur New Testament Commentary: Ephesians*. Chicago: Moody, 1986.
Nee, Watchman. *Sit, Walk, Stand*. 4th ed. Ft. Washington, PA: Christian Literature Crusade, 1962.
Phillips, J. B. *Letters to Young Churches*. New York: Macmillian, 1947.

Salmond, S. D. F. "The Epistle to the Ephesians." *The Expositor's Greek Testament.* Vol 3. W. Robertson Nicoll, ed. 1897-1910. Reprint, Grand Rapids: Eerdmans, 1983.

Seamands, David A. *Healing Grace.* Wheaton, IL: Scripture Press, 1988. This book has been reprinted several times including Light & Life Communications, 1999.

Sutcliffe, Joseph. *A Commentary on the Old and New Testament.* 2 vols. 1834. Reprint, Salem, OH: Allegheny, 2000.

Tasker, R. V. G. "Hope." *New Bible Dictionary.* 2nd ed. J. D. Douglas, ed. Wheaton, IL: Tyndale House, 1982.

Terry, Milton S. *Biblical Hermeneutics.* 2nd ed. 1885. Reprinted, Grand Rapids: Zondervan, 1974.

Trench, Richard C. *Synonyms of the New Testament.* 1880. Reprint, Grand Rapids: Eerdmans, 1953.

Tyerman, Luke. *The Life and Times of John Wesley.* 3 vols. London: Hodder & Stoughton, 1872.

__________. *Wesley's Designated Successor.* London: Hodder & Stoughton, 1882.

Walsh, Thomas. "The Whole Armor of God." 1759. *The Lives of Early Methodist Preachers.* 6 vols. 5th ed. Thomas Jackson, ed. London: Wesleyan Conference Office, 1865. 3:221-240.

Wesley, John. *Explanatory Notes Upon the New Testament.* 1754. Reprinted, Salem, OH: Schmul, 1976.

__________. *The Bicentennial Edition of the Works of John Wesley.* 35 vols. when complete; 26 volumes to date. Randy Maddox, ed. Nashville: Abingdon, 1976-. [*BE*]

www.ingramcontent.com/pod-product-compliance
Lightning Source LLC
LaVergne TN
LVHW011052110826
845149LV00015B/3470

9798993769684